MISSIONAL
COMMUNITY
STUDY GUIDE

BASED ON THE BOOK

SPIRITUAL MULTIPLICATION
IN THE REAL WORLD

MULTIPLICATION
PRESS

This study guide is based on the book *Spiritual Multiplication in the Real World* by Bob McNabb.

spiritualmultiplication.org

Spiritual Multiplication in the Real World: Missional Community Study Guide

Second Printing

ISBN 978-1-942374-01-5

CONTENTS

WHO SHOULD USE THIS STUDY GUIDE?

- Groups of six to twelve believers who are established in their walk with the Lord (Young believers who still need establishing in the faith would benefit more from being in a group that uses *Foundations: Missional Community Guidebook*.)

- Disciples who are ready to enter into the adventure of team evangelism and disciple-making

- People who are able to fulfill the requirements of the Team Covenant (next page)

WHAT ARE SOME OF THE MAJOR LEARNING OBJECTIVES OF THIS STUDY?

Participants will gain the following:

- A conviction for disciple-making efforts to be done in the context of a disciple-making team and movement as well as knowledge of the essential elements of a movement

- An understanding of the evangelism process and a commitment to practice those steps together with fellow teammates as part of a team evangelistic effort

- An overview of the disciple-making process and an understanding of how to move disciples from new birth to maturity to reproduction

HOW IS THIS STUDY GUIDE DIFFERENT FROM OTHER DISCIPLESHIP MATERIALS?

Most discipleship materials focus on knowledge acquisition. Their primary focus is to learn. The hope is that after learning, you will start doing. This study guide is different. The focus is on doing and building habits. As you build these habits, you will learn, and you will keep learning long after you finish these materials. The habits that you will work together to establish are:

- Daily Time with God (self-feeding on his Word)

- Evangelism

- Prayer for the Lost

- Scripture Memory

- Obedience

- Teamwork

INTRODUCTION

A MISSIONAL COMMUNITY IS A DISCIPLE-MAKING TEAM.

The term "Missional Community" has become very popular. Because of this, it is used to mean a wide variety of things. With this in mind, we have chosen to use the term "disciple-making team" frequently in these materials as a clarifying synonym for missional community.

HOW IS A DISCIPLE-MAKING TEAM DIFFERENT FROM A SMALL-GROUP?

The purpose of a disciple-making team is to glorify God by making disciples of all nations. Increasing our biblical knowledge is not the goal, but that will happen. The purpose is not to fellowship and pray, although we will do those things. Finally, the purpose is not to hold us accountable to spiritual disciplines, though that will occur when we meet. As you can see, a disciple-making team differs from a small group, a discipleship group, a Bible study, or a prayer group. Of course, there is nothing wrong with being a part of any of those types of groups.

Disciple-making teams are different in that they seek to stay focused on fulfilling the Great Commission through the multiplication of disciple-makers and new disciple-making teams. This focus drives members into deeper times of fellowship, prayer, Bible study, and accountability as the team lives and ministers together in a missional community. Mission is not one of the purposes of the team; it is the reason the team exists.

TEAM COVENANT

By God's grace, I covenant with the other members of my team to:

- Spend at least three hours with Jesus each week.
- Spend at least two hours reaching out to the lost each week.
- Spend at least one hour in prayer for my lost friends and the world with others of this team each week.
- Arrive prepared and ready to contribute to the group each weekly Half-Time meeting.
- Begin discipling others within a few months of completing this study.

I will strive, by the grace of God, to meet the above commitments.

Signed _KBlaster_ Date _2_ / _10_ / _15_

HOW CAN THIS GROUP DEVELOP LEADERS?

First, find an apprentice or co-leader who will help you lead the group. Hopefully, doing this with you will help prepare them to lead their own group soon.

Ideally, there will be at least two or three people out of the six to twelve in the group whom you can challenge to join as your apprentices.

The best people to consider for this are ones who:

- Have been established in their faith
- Have displayed faithfulness in passing on what they are taught
- Are teachable to you
- Have the availability to help you lead the group

Your strategy should be to spend extra time with these apprentices (like Jesus did with Peter, James, and John) and equip them to help lead the others in the community. This gets you discipling people in the context of ministry.

HOW TO CHALLENGE SOMEONE INTO THIS GROUP

PRAY AND ASK GOD TO BRING TO MIND THE NAMES OF SIX TO TWELVE PEOPLE WHO:

- Are already established in their faith
- Seem eager to evangelize and make disciples

SCHEDULE AN APPOINTMENT WITH THOSE YOU WILL CHALLENGE ONTO THE TEAM.

- Use the Sharing the Vision tool (p. 125)
- Go over the Purpose page and Team Covenant
- Take along one of your apprentices if possible

SET A DATE BY WHICH THEY MUST DECIDE.

WEEKLY 3-2-1

3 HOURS with Jesus

Everything begins with God. The foundation of a healthy personal ministry must be our own relationship with Christ. Therefore, commit to communing with him through prayer, worship, and reading his Word at least three hours a week.

2 HOURS with the lost

In order to reap, we must sow the seed of the gospel. We will spend at least two hours a week finding lost people, generating interest in Jesus, sharing the gospel, and Lord willing, helping them decide to follow Christ. Jesus sent his disciples two-by-two. In the same way, we want to go out two-by-two with other people on our team. We may not share the gospel every time, but we will always do something evangelistic, like meeting new people, sharing our testimonies, praying for people's needs, or inviting them to experience our community.

1 HOUR with each other in prayer

Jesus informs us that the key to the harvest is prayer. To see people enter into the Kingdom of God, we must become a people dedicated to prayer both privately and corporately. As a community, we will dedicate at least one hour of corporate prayer for the lost and the nations each week.

WEEKLY HALF-TIME MEETINGS

When it comes to spiritual multiplication, what happens all week long is more important than what happens in a once-a-week meeting. That's why we call our meetings "Half-Time." They're simply an opportunity to pause once a week and report on what God has been doing in the last six days, pray and encourage one another, plan our next week of ministry, and discuss the week's reading assignments. The components of each meeting are explained below.

WELCOME || 15 minutes

The Welcome portion will provide an opportunity to learn about the others in our community. Each week, we will have a different icebreaker question to discuss.

WITNESS || 10 minutes

The Witness time is an opportunity to share about what God did the previous week in our personal lives or in the lives of our family and friends. (Testimonies of what happened with our lost friends will occur during the Works section.) Be sure to write down a few notes in your workbook so you can look back and remember what God has done.

WORSHIP || 10 minutes

The Worship time is for our group to pray, sing, talk, or praise God in any other way that seems fitting to worship him for who he is and what he has done.

WORKS || 25 minutes

The Works time is for our group to share about what God is doing among our lost friends and plan for the next week's ministry.

Each week, we will write names of our lost friends on a large piece of light blue poster board or fabric called "Big Blue." (You can read "The Legend of Big Blue" on p. 122.) Names should only be added once you have a person's phone number and are likely to see them again. We will underline names of friends we are studying the Bible with and put a cross next to any people who start following Christ.

We will also start adding some of these names to our FISHing charts (p. 118) as we begin to share with them.

We will share how our ministry went in the past week and talk about any plans we need to make for the upcoming week.

We will then spend time in prayer for our lost friends and our plans for the week.

WORLD || 10 minutes

The World time will help us learn a little more about the world in which we live. Each week, the "Know God's World" section will provide a few facts about the world. In the "Share Helpful Resources" section, a different team member will take responsibility for learning about the resource of the week and then share about it with the team. We will choose one person to research and share for the next week. We will finish the World time in prayer for the nations.

WORD || 20 minutes

The Word time gives our community an opportunity to discuss the "Daily Quiet Times" and the "Learning Questions" from *Spiritual Multiplication in the Real World* from the previous week. This time will also be used to review the "Key Verse."

GAME PLAN

This is a convenient list of everything we need to do before next week's Half-Time. We will use this to keep track of assignments and set goals.

LEARNING QUESTIONS

Each week, we will be assigned one or two chapters from the book *Spiritual Multiplication in the Real World*. There are questions in this workbook that will help guide our learning and discussion. We will complete our reading and answer the questions before we show up to Half-Time each week.

DAILY QUIET TIMES

Each week, we will have a set of Daily Quiet Times to guide our three hours of time with God. These readings go along with the topics of *Spiritual Multiplication in the Real World*. Each of us should read the verses in context to get the full picture of what is being said.

KEY VERSE

These are important verses that come from our weekly readings. Each week, we will memorize the assigned verse and be prepared to recite it at the Half-Time meeting.

WEEK ONE

Introduction Meeting

WELCOME II 15 MINUTES

Have everyone introduce themselves by
answering these questions:
    What is your name?
    Why do you want to be in a disciple-
    making team?

Take some time to familiarize yourselves
with this entire workbook.

Read through together and discuss the
Introduction (p. 1-6).

Sign the Covenant (p. 2).

WITNESS II 10 MINUTES

What did you see God do this week?

WORSHIP II 10 MINUTES

Thank God together in prayer for what he
did last week.

Use an iPod, guitar, etc. and sing a few
songs together.

WORKS II 25 MINUTES

FISHING CHART
Turn to the FISHing chart (p. 118). Take
a few minutes to write down the names
of your lost friends and relatives who live
in the same town as you. If you don't have
ten, then make a plan to meet new people
this week.

BIG BLUE
As a group, write the names of your lost
friends on the large piece of poster board
or fabric we are calling "Big Blue." After
all the names are written, circle around
and pray for your friends.

TOOLS
The leader should introduce "My Story:
Interest-Creating Testimony" (p. 120)
and then demonstrate how to share it by
telling their own using the outline. You
will be working on your story throughout
this week and will practice sharing it at
Half-Time next week.

ACTIVITY
Turn to the Game Plan on the next page
and fill in your goals for this week.

GAME PLAN FOR NEXT WEEK

3 HOURS *with Jesus*

Daily Quiet Times
Memorize Key Verse: Mark 4:20

2 HOURS *with lost people*

If your FISHing chart is not full, meet new people
I will meet _____ new people this week

1 HOUR *with each other in prayer*

This week I will pray with _____

LEARNING ASSIGNMENT

Complete "My Story: Creating Interest Testimony" worksheet (p. 120)
Read *Spiritual Multiplication in the Real World* (Ch. 1-2) and answer the
Learning Questions

WEEK TWO

KEY VERSE

Mark 4:20
But those that were sown on the good soil are the ones who hear the word and accept it and bear fruit, thirtyfold and sixtyfold and a hundredfold.

SPIRITUAL MULTIPLICATION IN THE REAL WORLD

WORD

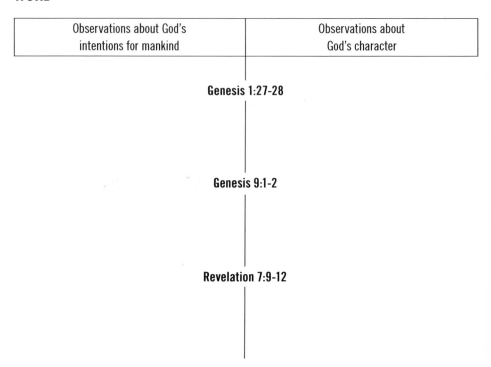

Observations about God's intentions for mankind	Observations about God's character

Genesis 1:27-28

Genesis 9:1-2

Revelation 7:9-12

WORSHIP

Praise God for what you saw about him in the Word today.

Today I thank God for...

I will worship God by obeying in the following ways this week:

Today I will trust God for...

▷ Learn this week's Key Verse.

WORD

Observations about God's promises		Observations about God's character
He has not withheld anything from us. They are powerful	Genesis 22:9-18	He is faithful to his promises
He has and will keep his promises	Hebrews 6:13-20	He is trustworthy We can put all of our hope in him, and he will never fail us.
He has already fulfilled them.	Galatians 3:7-9	He is smart and purposeful in all His ways.

How do the promises made to Abraham apply to you?

Describe the encouragement you find in these verses.

Write a specific life goal related to multiplication that you would like to trust God to accomplish through your life.

WORSHIP

Praise God for what you saw about him in the Word today.

Today I thank God for...

I will worship God by obeying in the following ways this week:

Today I will trust God for...

▷ Review this week's Key Verse.

13

DAILY QUIET TIMES II WEEK 2: DAY 3

WORD

Principles of spiritual multiplication observed	Observations about God's character
·do not be ashamed even in ~~the~~ persecution ·be willing to suffer for the sake of the Good News ★ This was His plan from the beginning ·He has chosen us as vessels	power, love, self discipline ·He does not abandon us.

2 Timothy 1

WORSHIP

Praise God for what you saw about him in the Word today.

Thank you that you are your servants are. ~~You do~~ not ~~intentional~~ as ~~the~~ abandon us, but you are always with us and with the body.

Today I thank God for...

The members of the body who care and love for me as a sister ~~o~~ in christ.

I will worship God by obeying in the following ways this week:

I will ~~do so~~ put more effort into serving and caring for your body and my commitments

Today I will trust God for...

Giving me strength and grace ~~to~~ when i feel that I'm in over my head.

▷ Review this week's Key Verse.   March 4:20

But those that were sown on the good soil are The ones ~~that~~ who hear the word, and accept it, and bear fruit, thirty fold, and 60 fold ✱ 100fold.

14

WORD Hebrews 12:1 Therefore since we have such a huge crowd of witnesses to the life of faith, let us strip off every weight that slows us down, esp. the sin that co easily trips us up.

Principles of spiritual multiplication observed	Observations about God's character
· teach truths to trustworthy people who will be able to pass them on.	Let us run w/ endurance the race God has set before us.
2 Timothy 2	
we share our suffering w/ Christ and all of the believers who have suffered for Christ.	He knows us. He is the truth and knows the truth.
1 Corinthians 4:14-17	
The WORD OF GOD CANNOT BE CHAINED	He has no part in evil, but His purpose is life.
It cannot be suppressed → it multiplies	He is patient but uncompromising.
	Ls even the rocks will praise Him.

WORSHIP

Praise God for what you saw about him in the Word today.

Thank you God for being so full of life. Thank you that your light shines in the darkness, we just have to believe that you are light and have faith in your Word.

Today I thank God for...

Being faithful and giving us His spirit to overcome. Thank you that you do not leave us where we are at, but you have a purpose for us.

I will worship God by obeying in the following ways this week:

I will spend time in prayer for those who are lost. I will turn my eyes to you and ask for your words.

Today I will trust God for...

my future.

▷ Review this week's Key Verse. But those that were sown on ~e good soil are those who hear the word, and ~ept it and bear fruit 30 fold, 60 fold, 100 fold. 15

WORD They will consider nothing sacred

Principles of spiritual multiplication observed	Observations about God's character
~~* Be prepared *~~ **2 Timothy 3 (especially verses 10-11)**	
• The Lords ways and ministry are opposed to the world & vise versa.	He is all in. He does not hold back or compromise.
• His ministry is loving & forgiving	
• He is multiplied when He is loved more than pleasure.	He has no fear in Him therefore we should have no fear.
• seek truth not knowledge.	

* Spiritual endurance
* wisdom is the knowledge of Jesus Christ.

WORSHIP * pour out our lives *

Praise God for what you saw about him in the Word today.

~~Psalm that~~ Praise you God that you are greater than the world. Praise you that you have overcome

Today I thank God for... and are seated on the throne.

The confidence we get to walk in as His children, and the opportunities to serve Him.

I will worship God by obeying in the following ways this week:

Praying for the body and allowing God to transform my thoughts.

Today I will trust God for...

Being present with me at all times.

▷ Review this week's Key Verse. But those that are sown on the good soil are those who hear the word, and accept i and bear fruit, 30fold, 60fold, 100 fold-

16

WORD

Principles of spiritual multiplication observed	Observations about God's character
✲ Be prepared ✲ · patience. · encourage · word based, not desire based. · fight, endure, remain faithful. · it is eternally minded	2 Timothy 4 He is ~~was~~ always ready to gift His believers with eternal life. He is our teacher and all that we need. His word, spirit and guidence.

WORSHIP

Praise God for what you saw about him in the Word today.

Praise you Lord that you are reality!
Praise you that you equipt us for your glory
and work.

Today I thank God for...

My parents and the people who have poured themselves out to me.

I will worship God by obeying in the following ways this week:

Asking the Lord how I may be his hands and feet.

Today I will trust God for...

Being my endurance and that He will speak thru ~~me~~. me

▷ Review this week's Key Verse.
But those ~~who~~ that are sown on the good soil are those who hear the word ccept it, and bear fruit 30 fold, 60 fold, 100 fold.

17

SUMMARY AND REFLECTION DAY

After looking over this week's quiet times, summarize what God has been teaching you.

What specific action will you take to apply what you have learned?

Did you really meet with Jesus this week, or did you just go through the motions?

WORSHIP

Praise God for what you saw about him in the Word this week.

Today I thank God for...

I will worship God by obeying in the following ways this week:

Today I will trust God for...

▷ Write out this week's Key Verse below:

SPIRITUAL MULTIPLICATION IN THE REAL WORLD (Chapters 1-2)

1. How did you answer the four questions from page 1:

   • Is it hard for you to believe God wants to multiply your life and make your spiritual descendants as numerous as the stars in the sky and the sand on the seashore? Why or why not?

   • What are you specifically asking God to do through your life?

   • How many men or women are you asking God to equip as multiplying disciples through you?

   • How many nations are you asking God to impact through you? Describe how reading about the doctrine of multiplication impacted you.

2. Spiritual multiplication is God's plan for reaching the world, and he has no Plan B. In light of this, how should we respond to failure in our efforts to multiply?

3. What lies do you think Satan wants Christians to believe about spiritual multiplication in the real world? What lies have you believed?

4. In light of God's awesome power, is there something big you want to trust God to do through your life this year?

5. What is your number one takeaway from reading Chapters 1-2?

WELCOME II 15 MINUTES

Have each person answer the question:

Who has had the greatest impact on your spiritual life?

Split into pairs and share your Interest-Creating Testimony with a partner, giving each other feedback on how to make your story more clear or interest-creating.

WITNESS II 10 MINUTES

What did you see God do this week?

WORSHIP II 10 MINUTES

Thank God together in prayer for what he did last week.

Use an iPod, guitar, etc. and sing a few songs together.

WORKS II 25 MINUTES

FISHING CHART

Turn to the FISHing chart (p. 118) and write names of your lost friends on it.

The ideal people to have on your FISHing Chart are people:

Whom you will be able to see repeatedly

Who would be open to your influence

Discuss as a team where and how each of you can meet people who fulfill the two criteria above.

It's okay if you can't fill the chart this week. You will be working as a team to fill in new people in the coming weeks.

Turn to p. 121 and read about asking questions, then decide how many people you will share your story with this week. Write it in the Game Plan.

BIG BLUE

Get out your Big Blue and write in the names of the new lost friends you met this week. When all the names have been written, put the list in the middle of the group and pray for those listed. Do not hurry this prayer time. It is the life blood of your ministry as a team and should therefore be central in each of your meetings.

ACTIVITY

Turn to the Game Plan on the next page and fill in your goals for this week.

WORLD II 10 MINUTES

KNOW GOD'S WORLD: Missionaries

Ninety-nine percent of believers live and work among the 60 percent of the world's population that already has the gospel.

Only 10 percent of missionaries work among the 40 percent of the world's population that is considered unreached.

Three out of every five non-Christians live beyond the reach of same-culture evangelism. Someone will have to intentionally cross cultural or language barriers to reach them.[1]

SHARE HELPFUL RESOURCES

Assign next week's resource: Global Prayer Digest (globalprayerdigest.org)

PRAY FOR THE NATIONS

WORD II 10 MINUTES

Share Mark 4:20 with a partner.

Discuss the major learning points and application steps from your Daily Quiet Times (Day 7).

Discuss your answers to the Learning Questions for *Spiritual Multiplication in the Real World* (Ch. 1-2).

Close with prayer.

GAME PLAN FOR NEXT WEEK

3 HOURS *with Jesus*

Daily Quiet Times
Memorize Key Verse: Acts 2:46-47

2 HOURS *with lost people*

If your FISHing chart is not full, meet new people.
I will meet _____ new people this week

Share your story
I will share my story with _____ people this week

My ministry partner this week will be _____

1 HOUR *with each other in prayer*

This week I will pray with _____

LEARNING ASSIGNMENT

Read *Spiritual Multiplication in the Real World* (Ch. 3-4) and answer the Learning Questions

WEEK THREE

Chapter 3: Trouble in Multiplication Paradise

Chapter 4: Soil

KEY VERSE

Acts 2:46-47
And day by day, attending the temple together and breaking bread in their homes, they received their food with glad and generous hearts, praising God and having favor with all the people. And the Lord added to their number day by day those who were being saved.

SPIRITUAL MULTIPLICATION IN THE REAL WORLD

WORD

Foundations for ministry that were laid	Observations about God's will and his ways
"one accord in prayer" — everyone together in prayer *Acts 1*	He is clear & consistant His scriptures had been fulfilled.

WORSHIP

Praise God for what you saw about him in the Word today.

Today I thank God for... closed doors, opened doors healing, faith, hope

I will worship God by obeying in the following ways this week:

I will believe his promises.

Today I will trust God for...

my future, the things I hold onto.

▷ Learn this week's Key Verse.

WORD ✱having grace w/ all people

Observations about living in community and disciple-making as a team	Ways in which God displayed his goodness
- we are all filled w/ the Holy spirit - we all have a part of the body. a special function - they supported each/o. - teach & fellowship together. - all things common ✱ Simplicity of heart ✱	Acts 2 - he allowed the disciples a chance to step up and proclaim his glory. - He gave His believers not only His spirit, but also each other.

WORSHIP

Praise God for what you saw about him in the Word today.

His body is one. We will share in joy with his believers.

Today I thank God for...

His faithfulness to His promises. How he moves. even when we are weak

I will worship God by obeying in the following ways this week:

① Not being lazy with the little things

Today I will trust God for...

taking care of me

▷ Review this week's Key Verse.

25

DAILY QUIET TIMES II WEEK 3: DAY 3

WORD

Observations about living in community and disciple-making as a team	Ways in which God displayed his goodness
• travel by 2 (in this case) • allow the scripture to teach • gospel driven.	Acts 3 • grace for ignorance. • healing • he refreshes if we repent • sent his son to bless us.

WORSHIP

Praise God for what you saw about him in the Word today.

Praise you Lord that your desire to bless us was serious business.

Today I thank God for...

blessings! freedom! Life! everything that Jesus died to give us.

I will worship God by obeying in the following ways this week:

Pressing into the person of Jesus! His Life not my own.

Today I will trust God for...

my personal life, I want to glorify him.

▷ Review this week's Key Verse.

26

24-31

WORD

Lifted up their voice w/ one accord

Observations about living in community and teamwork	Observations about Jesus
· ~~we~~ we are w/ Jesus. recognized as His w/ out education or self worth	· he moves thru the Holy Spirit
· We must speak the things of Jesus. ~~love~~ He is our ministry. not love, confidence, service but Jesus and his entirety.	· he is the cornerstone · He is <u>the only</u> name thru which we can be saved

WORSHIP · all things were common   heart & soul are one in the body.

Praise God for what you saw about him in the Word today.

Today I thank God for...

I will worship God by obeying in the following ways this week:

Today I will trust God for...

▷ Review this week's Key Verse.

WORD

Observations about the importance of unity	Observations about the attributes of God
-none is above another - we together answer to God above men.	- He is all knowing - He protects His people - He is unstoppable and above all human power.

Acts 5

John 17:20-23

Romans 15:5-9

WORSHIP

Praise God for what you saw about him in the Word today.

Today I thank God for...

I will worship God by obeying in the following ways this week:

Today I will trust God for...

▷ Review this week's Key Verse.

WORD

Benefits of teamwork	Observations about God's grace in suffering

Acts 6

WORSHIP

Praise God for what you saw about him in the Word today.

Today I thank God for...

I will worship God by obeying in the following ways this week:

Today I will trust God for...

▷ Review this week's Key Verse.

SUMMARY AND REFLECTION DAY

After looking over this week's quiet times, summarize what God has been teaching you.

He has been teaching me to speak boldly. He is carrying out His purpose through our bravery

What specific action will you take to apply what you have learned?

I want to pray for those the Lord wants me to pray for

Did you really meet with Jesus this week, or did you just go through the motions?

Both. I am learning how to balance my time and give it to the Lord in faith that He uses it better than I could.

WORSHIP

Praise God for what you saw about him in the Word this week.

He is just but he has set us up for success

Today I thank God for...

How he shines and the true joy he gives us. He doesn't ask the world of us

I will worship God by obeying in the following ways this week:

Pressing into the body and working together with them.

Today I will trust God for...

Sidney's salvation and future.

▷ Write out this week's Key Verse below:

And day by day, attending the temple together and breaking bread in their home, they recieved their food with glad and generous hearts, praising God and

SPIRITUAL MULTIPLICATION IN THE REAL WORLD (Chapters 3-4)

1. Have you ever tried to multiply spiritually? If so, how did it go?

I have never actively asked someone to learn about Christ.

2. Respond to the statement, "If you're not fishing, you're not following." Why do you agree or disagree?

I agree more and more every day. I am starting to understand that this is our purpose, because its what were here for. hence purpose.

3. Describe the type of group that you will need to be a part of if you are going to multiply your life consistently over the coming years.

I need to be a part of a group that keeps me accountable

4. What thoughts come to mind when you read about the impact your life could have if you too applied the biblical principles practiced by highly effective disciple-makers?

I feel encouraged and hopeful that the Lord will touch 1000s, maybe more, but discouraged that I dont know where to start.

5. How do you think American individualism has affected the way we think about disciple-making?

I don't rely on the body for nearly enough. It makes sense that we want to share life with others. He wants us to in a way of building up.

6. What specific action step do you need to take to apply what you learned in your reading this week?

Reach out to my peers in the group. Pray and ask in faith for those who lack, and where I lack.

WELCOME || 15 MINUTES

Have each person answer the question:

What is one book (besides the Bible) that has impacted your spiritual life?

Split into pairs and share your story with a new partner, giving each other feedback on how to make your story more clear or interest-creating.

WITNESS || 10 MINUTES

What did you see God do this week?

WORSHIP || 10 MINUTES

Thank God together in prayer for what he did last week.

Make a list of the names of God and praise him for his attributes.

WORKS || 25 MINUTES

FISHING CHART

Update your FISHing chart with any new people you met this week or steps you took in the FISHing process.

BIG BLUE

Add your team's new friends to Big Blue. Put the list in the middle of the group and pray over your friends.

ACTIVITY

Turn to p. 122 and read about a Matthew Party. Then spend some time as a group planning one together.

Turn to the Game Plan on the next page and fill in your goals for this week.

WORLD || 10 MINUTES

KNOW GOD'S WORLD: Money

Of foreign mission funding, 87 percent is used for work among those already Christian. Twelve percent of funding is spent for work among those who are already evangelized but non-Christians. One percent is used for work among unevangelized and unreached people.[1] According to the National Retail Federation, in 2011, Americans spent the same amount on Halloween costumes (for their pets!).

Do you know of ways that you can ensure that a more significant portion of your giving goes to reaching those who have never heard of Jesus?

SHARE HELPFUL RESOURCES

Report on this week's resource: Global Prayer Digest (globalprayerdigest.org)

Assign next week's resource: Finishing the Task (finishingthetask.com)

PRAY FOR THE NATIONS

WORD || 20 MINUTES

Share Acts 2:46-47 with a partner.

Discuss the major learning points and application steps from your Daily Quiet Times (Day 7).

Discuss your answers to the Learning Questions for *Spiritual Multiplication in the Real World* (Ch. 3-4).

Close with prayer.

GAME PLAN FOR NEXT WEEK

3 HOURS *with Jesus*

Daily Quiet Times
Memorize Key Verse: Hebrews 10:24-25

2 HOURS *with lost people*

If your FISHing chart is not full, meet new people and use the Interest-Creating
Questions.
I will meet _____1_____ new people this week

Share your story
I will share my story with __1__ people this week

My ministry partner this week will be _____ Wed night 7 pm

Plan a Matthew Party   Monday night ?

1 HOUR *with each other in prayer*

This week I will pray with _____

LEARNING ASSIGNMENT

Read *Spiritual Multiplication in the Real World* (Ch. 5) and answer the
Learning Questions

WEEK FOUR

Chapter 5: Essential Elements

KEY VERSE

Hebrews 10:24-25
And let us consider how to stir up one another to love and good works, not neglecting to meet together, as is the habit of some, but encouraging one another, and all the more as you see the Day drawing near.

DAILY QUIET TIMES II WEEK 4: DAY 1 *Complete my story*

WORD   *Ask Syd about Monday   P. 120*

Observations about vision and vision casting	Observations about the kingdom
	He has given us one purpose to pursue.
	Matthew 4:19
it is an eternal vision it takes faith.	Matthew 6:19-21 *It has to be our heart.*
	Matthew 13:1-52

What do you need to do to put yourself in a situation where you are consistently challenged with an eternal and multiplying vision?

Whom do you need to encourage this week, and how will you cast vision with them?

WORSHIP

Praise God for what you saw about him in the Word today.

Today I thank God for...
Sidney and how you moved in her

I will worship God by obeying in the following ways this week:
by not stressing over what I cannot handle but laying it before Him.

Today I will trust God for...

▷ Learn this week's Key Verse.

WORD

What do you observe regarding the role of modeling in spiritual multiplication?

John 13:15 We have a model in Christ

2 Thessalonians 3:9 a pattern learned from and thru Christ to shine Christ to others.

Titus 2:7-8 incorruption - presenting yourself in a life-giving manner.

1 Corinthians 4:16-17
our ways are in Christ, thru us.

1 Corinthians 11:1

What attribute of Christ do you most admire and want to model for those you disciple?

boldness to speak God's truth. His love and

WORSHIP
peace that surpasses all knowledge.

Praise God for what you saw about him in the Word today.

We have a model to live by, in us! Hallelujah!

Today I thank God for...

I will worship God by obeying in the following ways this week:

Today I will trust God for...

▷ Review this week's Key Verse.

WORD

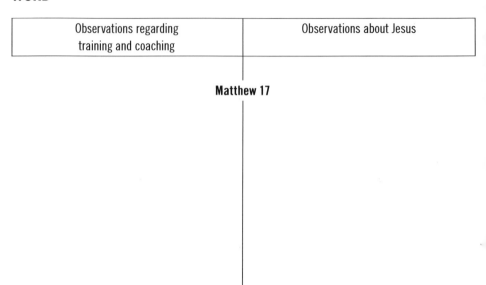

Observations regarding training and coaching	Observations about Jesus

Matthew 17

WORSHIP

Praise God for what you saw about him in the Word today.

Today I thank God for...

I will worship God by obeying in the following ways this week:

Today I will trust God for...

▷ Review this week's Key Verse.

WORD

Examples of Jesus' ministry to the masses	Examples of Jesus' ministry to the few

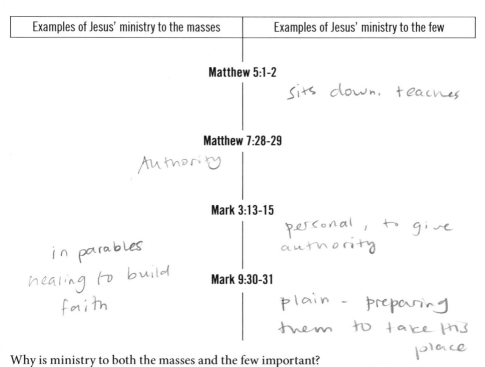

Matthew 5:1-2

sits down. teaches

Matthew 7:28-29

Authority

Mark 3:13-15

personal, to give authority

in parables
healing to build faith

Mark 9:30-31

plain - preparing them to take his place

Why is ministry to both the masses and the few important?

What relationship do you see between ministry to the masses and ministry to the few in spiritual multiplication?

Do you think you need to increase your ministry to the masses or the few? What steps will you take?

How do you see Jesus' love in his ministry to the masses and the few?

WORSHIP

Praise God for what you saw about him in the Word today.

Today I thank God for...

I will worship God by obeying in the following ways this week:

Today I will trust God for...

▷ Review this week's Key Verse.

WORD

Observations about their practice of prayer	Results of their prayers

steadfastly
together
unified

Acts 1:12-14   *three thousand saved*

Acts 2:41-3:10   *wonders & signs*

steadfast teaching & fellowship
community living

What steps will you take to devote yourself to prayer?

WORSHIP

Praise God for what you saw about him in the Word today.

Today I thank God for...

I will worship God by obeying in the following ways this week:

Today I will trust God for...

▷ Review this week's Key Verse.

WORD

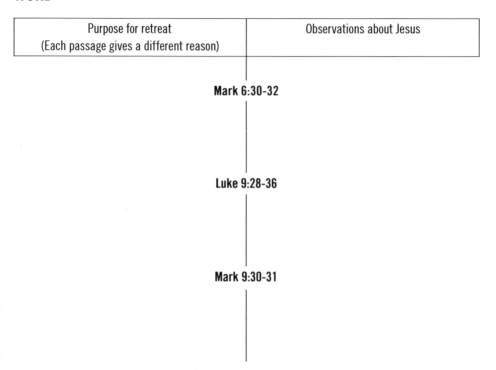

Purpose for retreat (Each passage gives a different reason)	Observations about Jesus
Mark 6:30-32	
Luke 9:28-36	
Mark 9:30-31	

Do you need to plan a retreat soon? For what purpose?

WORSHIP

Praise God for what you saw about him in the Word today.

Today I thank God for...

I will worship God by obeying in the following ways this week:

Today I will trust God for...

▷ Review this week's Key Verse.

SUMMARY AND REFLECTION DAY

After looking over this week's quiet times, summarize what God has been teaching you.

What specific action will you take to apply what you have learned?

Did you really meet with Jesus this week, or did you just go through the motions?

WORSHIP

Praise God for what you saw about him in the Word this week.

Today I thank God for...

I will worship God by obeying in the following ways this week:

Today I will trust God for...

▷ Write out this week's Key Verse below:

SPIRITUAL MULTIPLICATION IN THE REAL WORLD (Chapter 5)

1. What are the differences between a church that is designed to grow in attendance and one that is designed to equip and help its members multiply their lives?

The leader sets a vision. one may feed the body, but if we are not being equipted to multiply we are not working and growing as the body.

2. Why is it so important to be part of a church that possesses the seven essential elements of a disciple-making movement?

The essential elements are necessary and they worth the time for the building up of believers while at the same time multiplying. All out of the overflow of Jesus.

3. What do you think the author is saying are the main differences between a standard small group and a disciple-making team?

A disciple making small group focuses their eyes on Jesus and His purposeful glory. In turn Jesus works in us internally and guides us / convicts us in walking out our personal faith.

4. What is your major takeaway from this chapter? How will you apply what you learned?

I really took away the importance of fellowship with believers to further the kingdom. I want to ask the Lord to give me that passion for Him and His kingdom to overflow in my thoughts and actions.

WELCOME II 15 MINUTES

Have each person answer the question:

Who do you know that most models the vision of spiritual multiplication? Why did you pick this person?

Split into pairs and share your story with a new partner, giving each other feedback on how to make your story more clear or interest-creating.

WITNESS II 10 MINUTES

What did you see God do this week?

WORSHIP II 10 MINUTES

Thank God together in prayer for what he did last week.

Read Psalm 136 responsively: one person reads the first half of a verse, and everyone reads the second half together.

WORKS II 25 MINUTES

FISHING CHART
Update your FISHing chart with any new people you met this week or steps you took in the FISHing process.

BIG BLUE
Add your team's new friends to Big Blue. Put the list in the middle of the group and pray over your friends.

ACTIVITY
Turn to the Game Plan on the next page and fill in your goals for this week.

WORLD II 10 MINUTES

KNOW GOD'S WORLD: 10/40 Window

Eighty-six percent of all unreached people groups lie within the region called the 10/40 window, which is between 10 and 40 degrees north latitude, from the west coast of Africa to the east coast of Asia.[2]

These people are not "more lost" than your unsaved neighbor or family member, but they are "unreached" in the sense that they have not had the opportunity to hear the Gospel.[4]

SHARE HELPFUL RESOURCES
Report on this week's resource: Finishing the Task (finishingthetask.com)

Assign next week's resource: Open Doors (opendoors.org)

PRAY FOR THE NATIONS

WORD II 20 MINUTES

Share Hebrews 10:24-25 with a partner.

Discuss the major learning points and application steps from your Daily Quiet Times (Day 7).

Discuss your answers to the Learning Questions for *Spiritual Multiplication in the Real World* (Ch. 5).

Close with prayer.

GAME PLAN FOR NEXT WEEK

3 HOURS *with Jesus*

Daily Quiet Times
Memorize Key Verse: John 13:35

2 HOURS *with lost people*

If your FISHing chart is not full, meet new people and use the Interest-Creating Questions.
I will meet _____ new people this week

Share your story
I will share my story with _____ people this week

My ministry partner this week will be _____

1 HOUR *with each other in prayer*

This week I will pray with _____

LEARNING ASSIGNMENT

Read *Spiritual Multiplication in the Real World* (Ch. 6) and answer the Learning Questions

WEEK FIVE

Chapter 6: Gone Fishing

KEY VERSE

John 13:35
By this all people will know that you are my disciples, if you have love for one another.

DAILY QUIET TIMES || WEEK 5: DAY 1

WORD

Observations about evangelism	How Jesus created interest
The harvest is ready for reaping *John 4:1-45*	He related at her level
Jesus shares the good news that the savior has come.	· listened to the spirit
The time for the harvest is now.	

What do you observe about Jesus in this passage that impresses you?

He is so confident in His identity and not boastful about it.

WORSHIP

Praise God for what you saw about him in the Word today.

Lord thank you that we get to worship you in spirit and in truth. You do not distinguish

Today I thank God for... us as Jew or not Jew.

Lord thank you for rest. for slowing me down and reminding me what is important

I will worship God by obeying in the following ways this week:

I want to walk in confidence of The gospel and be aware of the Lord's harvest.

Today I will trust God for...

Sidney's salvation and my mom. Lord I trust you that you have prepared me for the harvest.

▷ Learn this week's Key Verse.

By this all people will know That you are my disciples, if you have love for one another

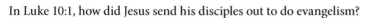

WORD

In Luke 10:1, how did Jesus send his disciples out to do evangelism?

2 by 2

What advantages do you see in approaching evangelism as a team rather than as individuals?

    John 13:34-35

    1 Corinthians 14:24-25

In light of these verses, what changes will you make to how you evangelize?

WORSHIP

Praise God for what you saw about him in the Word today.

Today I thank God for...

I will worship God by obeying in the following ways this week:

Today I will trust God for...

▷ Review this week's Key Verse.

WORD

Observations about evangelism	Observations about God

Acts 17:16-31

Finding out about people

Interesting people in the gospel

Sharing the good news

Helping people make a decision

In light of these verses, what changes will you make to how you evangelize?

WORSHIP

Praise God for what you saw about him in the Word today.

Today I thank God for...

I will worship God by obeying in the following ways this week:

Today I will trust God for...

▷ Review this week's Key Verse.

WORD

Observations about evangelism	Observations about God

1 Corinthians 3:1-23

WORSHIP

Praise God for what you saw about him in the Word today.

Today I thank God for...

I will worship God by obeying in the following ways this week:

Today I will trust God for...

▷ Review this week's Key Verse.

WORD

Observations about evangelism	Observations about Jesus

Matthew 11:25-30

Observations about creating interest

Observations about calling people to a decision

WORSHIP

Praise God for what you saw about him in the Word today.

Today I thank God for...

I will worship God by obeying in the following ways this week:

Today I will trust God for...

▷ Review this week's Key Verse.

WORD

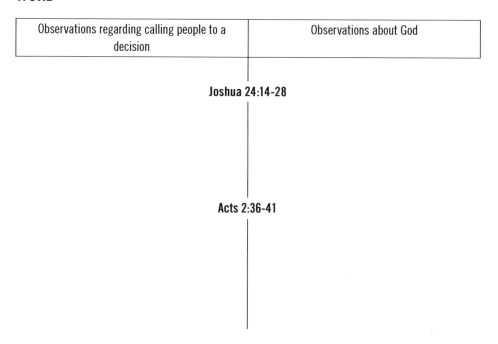

Observations regarding calling people to a decision	Observations about God

Joshua 24:14-28

Acts 2:36-41

Is there someone you need to invite to follow Jesus this week?

WORSHIP

Praise God for what you saw about him in the Word today.

Today I thank God for...

I will worship God by obeying in the following ways this week:

Today I will trust God for...

▷ Review this week's Key Verse.

SUMMARY AND REFLECTION DAY

After looking over this week's quiet times, summarize what God has been teaching you.

What specific action will you take to apply what you have learned?

Did you really meet with Jesus this week, or did you just go through the motions?

WORSHIP

Praise God for what you saw about him in the Word this week.

Today I thank God for...

I will worship God by obeying in the following ways this week:

Today I will trust God for...

▷ Write out this week's Key Verse below:

SPIRITUAL MULTIPLICATION IN THE REAL WORLD (Chapter 6)

1. What was something new you learned from your reading this week?

2. Evaluate yourself in the following areas and share your answers with the group.
   (1 = Weakness, 3 = Average, 5 = Strength)

   _____ Finding new people with whom to share the gospel

   _____ Finding out about people's lives (asking good questions)

   _____ Creating interest

   _____ Sharing the Gospel

   _____ Helping people make a decision and deal with barriers

3. What steps will you take to grow in your weak areas?

WELCOME II 15 MINUTES

Have each person answer the question:

What is the best news you have ever heard (besides the gospel)?

How long did it take you to start telling others about your good news?

Split into pairs and share your story with a new partner, giving each other feedback on how to make your story more clear or interest-creating.

WITNESS II 10 MINUTES

What did you see God do this week?

WORSHIP II 10 MINUTES

Thank God together in prayer for what he did last week.

Have a time of silence before the Lord to hear his voice and worship. Ask him to bring to mind a verse you could use to worship him or encourage the group. Pray the verse back to the Lord.

WORKS II 25 MINUTES

FISHING CHART

Update your FISHing chart with any new people you met this week or steps you took in the FISHing process.

BIG BLUE

Add your team's new friends to Big Blue. Put the list in the middle of the group and pray over your friends.

ACTIVITY

Turn to the Game Plan on the next page and fill in your goals for this week.

WORLD II 10 MINUTES

KNOW GOD'S WORLD: Tribals

There are 161 million people in 704 tribal people groups.[1]

They have animistic and superstitious beliefs (everything has a spirit, such as water, rocks, trees, animals).

They must be careful not to offend these spirits and must appease them with sacrifices.

They often worship idols and ancestors and visit witch doctors.

SHARE HELPFUL RESOURCES

Report on this week's resource: Open Doors (opendoors.org)

Assign next week's resource: Voice of the Martyrs (persecution.org)

PRAY FOR THE NATIONS

WORD II 20 MINUTES

Share John 13:35 with a partner.

Discuss the major learning points and application steps from your Daily Quiet Times (Day 7).

Discuss your answers to the Learning Questions for *Spiritual Multiplication in the Real World* (Ch. 6).

Close with prayer.

GAME PLAN FOR NEXT WEEK

3 HOURS *with Jesus*

Daily Quiet Times
Memorize Key Verse: 1 Thessalonians 2:7-8

2 HOURS *with lost people*

I will create interest with **Hannah B.** (person on FISHing chart) by doing **walking** (interest-creating activity).

My ministry partner this week will be _____

1 HOUR *with each other in prayer*

This week I will pray with _____

LEARNING ASSIGNMENT

Read *Spiritual Multiplication in the Real World* (Ch. 7) and answer the Learning Questions

WEEK SIX

Chapter 7: Parenthood

KEY VERSE

1 Thessalonians 2:7-8
But we were gentle among you, like a nursing mother taking care of her own children. So, being affectionately desirous of you, we were ready to share with you not only the gospel of God but also our own selves, because you had become very dear to us.

WORD

Observations about discipling relationships	Observations about God

1 Thessalonians 1

WORSHIP

Praise God for what you saw about him in the Word today.

Today I thank God for...

I will worship God by obeying in the following ways this week:

Today I will trust God for...

▷ Learn this week's Key Verse.

WORD

Observations about discipling relationships	Observations about God

1 Thessalonians 2

WORSHIP

Praise God for what you saw about him in the Word today.

Today I thank God for...

I will worship God by obeying in the following ways this week:

Today I will trust God for...

▷ Review this week's Key Verse.

WORD

Observations about discipling relationships	Observations about God

1 Thessalonians 3

WORSHIP

Praise God for what you saw about him in the Word today.

Today I thank God for...

I will worship God by obeying in the following ways this week:

Today I will trust God for...

▷ Review this week's Key Verse.

WORD

Observations about discipling relationships	Observations about God

1 Thessalonians 4

WORSHIP

Praise God for what you saw about him in the Word today.

Today I thank God for...

I will worship God by obeying in the following ways this week:

Today I will trust God for...

▷ Review this week's Key Verse.

DAILY QUIET TIMES II WEEK 6: DAY 5

WORD

Observations about discipling relationships	Observations about God

1 Thessalonians 5

WORSHIP

Praise God for what you saw about him in the Word today.

Today I thank God for...

I will worship God by obeying in the following ways this week:

Today I will trust God for...

▷ Review this week's Key Verse.

WORD

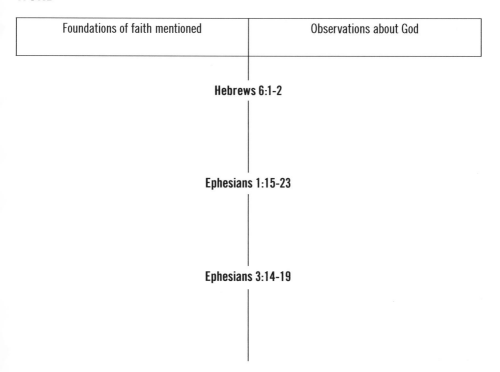

Foundations of faith mentioned	Observations about God

Hebrews 6:1-2

Ephesians 1:15-23

Ephesians 3:14-19

WORSHIP

Praise God for what you saw about him in the Word today.

Today I thank God for...

I will worship God by obeying in the following ways this week:

Today I will trust God for...

▷ Review this week's Key Verse.

SUMMARY AND REFLECTION DAY

After looking over this week's quiet times, summarize what God has been teaching you.

What specific action will you take to apply what you have learned?

Did you really meet with Jesus this week, or did you just go through the motions?

WORSHIP

Praise God for what you saw about him in the Word this week.

Today I thank God for...

I will worship God by obeying in the following ways this week:

Today I will trust God for...

▷ Write out this week's Key Verse below:

SPIRITUAL MULTIPLICATION IN THE REAL WORLD (Chapter 7)

1. What are the needs of a new disciple?

    accountability

    encouragement

    mentor

2. What are some of the key things a disciple-maker can do to help a new believer become established in the faith?

    5 F's

    Community

3. What are some traps to avoid when establishing new believers?

4. Why does the author discourage discipling someone one-on-one?

    to prevent heresy

5. What specific application steps do you believe you need to take in light of what you read in this chapter?

6. With whom will you share what you learned in this chapter?

WELCOME || 15 MINUTES

Share a story of an answered prayer.

WITNESS || 10 MINUTES

What did you see God do this week?

WORSHIP || 10 MINUTES

Thank God together in prayer for what he did last week.

Use an iPod, guitar, etc. and sing a few songs together.

WORKS || 25 MINUTES

FISHING CHART

Update your FISHing chart with any new people you met this week or steps you took in the FISHing process.

BIG BLUE

Add your team's new friends to Big Blue. Put the list in the middle of the group and pray over your friends.

TOOLS

The leader should introduce "The Bridge Illustration" (p. 123) and then demonstrate how to share it.

Pair up and practice The Bridge with another teammate, giving each other feedback.

ACTIVITY

Plan another Matthew Party as a group.

Turn to the Game Plan on the next page and fill in your goals for this week.

WORLD || 10 MINUTES

KNOW GOD'S WORLD: Hindus

There are 860 million people in 1,843 Hindu people groups.[1]

They believe in millions of gods.

They worship idols of clay, stone, or pictures by giving them food, flowers, and money.

They believe they are caught in a cycle of birth-death-rebirth called reincarnation.

SHARE HELPFUL RESOURCES

Report on this week's resource: Voice of the Martyrs (persecution.org)

Assign next week's resource: Perspectives on the World Christian Movement (perspectives.org)

PRAY FOR THE NATIONS

WORD || 20 MINUTES

Share 1 Thessalonians 2:7-8 with a partner.

Discuss the major learning points and application steps from your Daily Quiet Times (Day 7).

Discuss your answers to the Learning Questions for *Spiritual Multiplication in the Real World* (Ch. 7).

Close with prayer.

GAME PLAN FOR NEXT WEEK

3 HOURS *with Jesus*

Daily Quiet Times
Memorize Key Verse: Ephesians 4:11-12

2 HOURS *with lost people*

Plan a Matthew Party

Share The Bridge
I will share The Bridge with _____ people this week

My ministry partner this week will be _____

1 HOUR *with each other in prayer*

This week I will pray with _____

LEARNING ASSIGNMENT

Read *Spiritual Multiplication in the Real World* (Ch. 8) and answer the
Learning Questions

WEEK SEVEN

Chapter 8: Learning to Fly

KEY VERSE

Ephesians 4:11-12
And he gave the apostles, the prophets, the evangelists, the shepherds and teachers, to equip the saints for the work of ministry, for building up the body of Christ,

WORD

Disciple-making and equipping observations	Observations about God

1 Timothy 1

WORSHIP

Praise God for what you saw about him in the Word today.

Today I thank God for...

I will worship God by obeying in the following ways this week:

Today I will trust God for...

▷ Learn this week's Key Verse.

WORD

Disciple-making and equipping observations	Observations about God

1 Timothy 2

WORSHIP

Praise God for what you saw about him in the Word today.

Today I thank God for...

I will worship God by obeying in the following ways this week:

Today I will trust God for...

▷ Review this week's Key Verse.

WORD

Disciple-making and equipping observations	Observations about God

1 Timothy 3

WORSHIP

Praise God for what you saw about him in the Word today.

Today I thank God for...

I will worship God by obeying in the following ways this week:

Today I will trust God for...

▷ Review this week's Key Verse.

WORD

Disciple-making and equipping observations	Observations about God

1 Timothy 4

WORSHIP

Praise God for what you saw about him in the Word today.

Today I thank God for...

I will worship God by obeying in the following ways this week:

Today I will trust God for...

▷ Review this week's Key Verse.

WORD

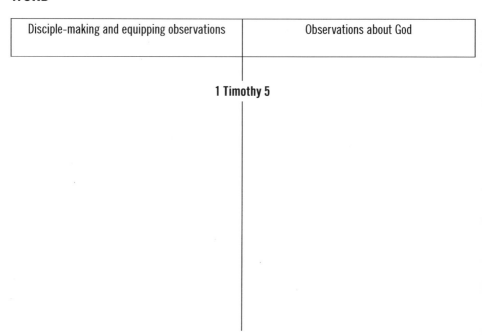

Disciple-making and equipping observations	Observations about God

1 Timothy 5

WORSHIP

Praise God for what you saw about him in the Word today.

Today I thank God for...

I will worship God by obeying in the following ways this week:

Today I will trust God for...

▷ Review this week's Key Verse.

WORD

Disciple-making and equipping observations	Observations about God

1 Timothy 6

WORSHIP

Praise God for what you saw about him in the Word today.

Today I thank God for...

I will worship God by obeying in the following ways this week:

Today I will trust God for...

▷ Review this week's Key Verse.

SUMMARY AND REFLECTION DAY

After looking over this week's quiet times, summarize what God has been teaching you.

What specific action will you take to apply what you have learned?

Did you really meet with Jesus this week, or did you just go through the motions?

WORSHIP

Praise God for what you saw about him in the Word this week.

Today I thank God for...

I will worship God by obeying in the following ways this week:

Today I will trust God for...

▷ Write out this week's Key Verse below:

SPIRITUAL MULTIPLICATION IN THE REAL WORLD (Chapter 8)

1. What is the best example of equipping you have ever seen?

2. What areas of your life are not good models for others?

3. Summarize what you believe were the author's major points regarding selection.

4. Do you agree or disagree with the author's emphasis on character development in the equipping stage of ministry? Why?

5. What is still unclear to you about the equipping phase of ministry?

6. What specific application steps do you believe you need to take in light of what you read in this chapter?

7. With whom will you share what you learned in this chapter?

WELCOME II 15 MINUTES

What have you found to be most helpful in spending quality time alone fellowshipping with God?

WITNESS II 10 MINUTES

What did you see God do this week?

WORSHIP II 10 MINUTES

Thank God together in prayer for what he did last week.

As a group, write down a list of as many of God's attributes as you can.

WORKS II 25 MINUTES

FISHING CHART
Update your FISHing chart with any new people you met this week or steps you took in the FISHing process.

BIG BLUE
Add your team's new friends to Big Blue. Put the list in the middle of the group and pray over your friends.

TOOLS
Pair up and practice The Bridge with another teammate, giving each other feedback.

ACTIVITY
Turn to the Game Plan on the next page and fill in your goals for this week.

WORLD II 10 MINUTES

KNOW GOD'S WORLD: Unreligious

There are 121 million people in 15 Unreligious people groups.[1]

They are mostly atheistic, with some remnants of ancestor worship or Buddhist beliefs.

Many have Communist governments that tell people there is no God.

The majority lives in the country of China.

SHARE HELPFUL RESOURCES
Report on this week's resource: Perspectives on the World Christian Movement (perspectives.org)

Assign next week's resource: Launch Global (launchglobal.org)

PRAY FOR THE NATIONS

WORD II 20 MINUTES

Share Ephesians 4:11-12 with a partner.

Discuss the major learning points and application steps from your Daily Quiet Times (Day 7).

Discuss your answers to the Learning Questions for *Spiritual Multiplication in the Real World* (Ch. 8).

Close with prayer.

GAME PLAN FOR NEXT WEEK

3 HOURS *with Jesus*

Daily Quiet Times
Memorize Key Verse: Matthew 9:37-38

2 HOURS *with lost people*

Share The Bridge
I will share The Bridge with _____ people this week

My ministry partner this week will be _____

1 HOUR *with each other in prayer*

This week I will pray with _____

LEARNING ASSIGNMENT

Read *Spiritual Multiplication in the Real World* (Ch. 9) and answer the
Learning Questions

WEEK EIGHT

Chapter 9: The Lost Aspect of Disciple-Making

KEY VERSE

Matthew 9:37-38
Then he said to his disciples, "The harvest is plentiful, but the laborers are few; therefore pray earnestly to the Lord of the harvest to send out laborers into his harvest."

WORD

Observations about God's heart for the nations	General observations about God's character
his deeds are among all nations	*Psalm 96* his deeds are wondrous
~ all people	He is powerful, creator, strength, beauty
- He will be glorified by the nations	His hand is over the entire earth.
· he welcomes us to his courts	He IS GREAT
He reigns	he is righteous
He judges with equity	

WORSHIP

Praise God for what you saw about him in the Word today.

Lord I see how overwhelmingly great you are. You are greater than this world, but you come to us.

Today I thank God for...

the body of Christ, and your constant prescence. The desire to walk with you.

I will worship God by obeying in the following ways this week:

Keeping your praise on our lips.

Today I will trust God for...

Davis. bless him Lord and show yourself to him.

▷ Learn this week's Key Verse.

WORD

Observations about God's heart for the nations	General observations about God's character

This is the gospel of His kingdom

Matthew 9:35-38

He is compassionate

He is faithful to many

He is the shepherd of all nations

he will finish his work,

prayer is important for the workers as well as the harvest.

and thats His heart desire.

He is selfless - He loves us so deeply, but never stops pursuing the lost sheep. It is his desire.

WORSHIP

Praise God for what you saw about him in the Word today.

That his heart is selfless.

Today I thank God for...

His growing desire in my heart.

I will worship God by obeying in the following ways this week:

Seeking his sheep. being obedient to His spirit.

Today I will trust God for...

My energy to press on and do my best with the time given.

▷ Review this week's Key Verse.

DAILY QUIET TIMES II WEEK 8: DAY 3

WORD

Observations about God's heart for the nations	General observations about God's character
He has made it so simple for us	Romans 10:5-17 · all encompassing
ANYONE who believes in him is forgiven	· 100% forgiveness for all people, no matter what, if they believe into him.
— will never be put to shame	— he has entrusted us w/ a job or a purpose
· All nations have been ushered in —	He supplies us complete.
Richly blesses all who call on him	

WORSHIP

Praise God for what you saw about him in the Word today.

Today I thank God for...

I will worship God by obeying in the following ways this week:

Today I will trust God for...

▷ Review this week's Key Verse.

WORD

Observations about God's heart for the nations	General observations about God's character
We are of one mind one voice **Romans 15** - Sing the praises of this name to the Gentiles we are ushered in w/ His people Hallelujah! He commands us to be a minister to the gentiles	He bears all oppression - it is not a set back b/c he is victorious · Ruler of the nations · fills us with his joy and hope - to over flow. · he gives understanding sight It is his will for his name to be proclaimed.

WORSHIP

Praise God for what you saw about him in the Word today.

Today I thank God for...

I will worship God by obeying in the following ways this week:

Today I will trust God for...

▷ Review this week's Key Verse.

WORD

Observations about God's heart for the nations	General observations about God's character
All prayers are heard **Revelation 5** He has purchased us with His blood. We are bought with a perfect price. Every one of us.	Jesus is worthy! He has triumphed He is just and has proven His love for us. He deserves all praise

WORSHIP

Praise God for what you saw about him in the Word today.

Today I thank God for...

I will worship God by obeying in the following ways this week:

Today I will trust God for...

▷ Review this week's Key Verse.

WORD

Observations about God's heart for the nations	Observations about the different ways God may give guidance for missions
2 Timothy 4:9-12	He gives us partners for ministry
Titus 1:5	He gives us a task and may keep us stable in one spot but has
Acts 16:1-10	a task of building disciples before us. ~~He gives us guidelines~~ We are lead by the Holy Spirit. He speaks to us and we just have to obey.

WORSHIP

Praise God for what you saw about him in the Word today.

Today I thank God for...

I will worship God by obeying in the following ways this week:

Today I will trust God for...

▷ Review this week's Key Verse.

SUMMARY AND REFLECTION DAY

After looking over this week's quiet times, summarize what God has been teaching you.

He is teaching me that he has bought us with a price. We have recieved his spirit and he sends us out to collect those that he has bought and whom he loves

What specific action will you take to apply what you have learned?

I will press into His holy spirit and act to glorify God, not just tip toe around Him.

Did you really meet with Jesus this week, or did you just go through the motions?

I did meet w/ Jesus.

WORSHIP

Praise God for what you saw about him in the Word this week.

His faithfulness and his humanity

Today I thank God for...

health and community

I will worship God by obeying in the following ways this week:

trusting His plan for my life when life is busy and I have so many questions.

Today I will trust God for...

His hand on my life, His perfect plan for me that I want to submit to

▷ Write out this week's Key Verse below:

SPIRITUAL MULTIPLICATION IN THE REAL WORLD (Chapter 9)

1. What do you think has caused such a great imbalance of laborers in the world today?

I think we have a mental block that there are different kinds of christians and their roles, but if we put aside culture and 'proffession' God has called us to one purpose

2. Why do you think most disciple-makers and church leaders are not more actively mobilizing their people to the unreached?

I think we often try to fix things internally ourselves when God does the work internally as we step out in faith and into the unknown. He is alive and working to strengthen the church, but wants our gaze to be outward

3. What new things did you learn from this chapter?

The importance of the body choosing who is sent - we do not have to worry where we go.

4. Is there anything in your life that is keeping you from successfully mobilizing laborers?

I dont know how to successfully make disciples (that i've experienced) to have the weight to ask that of someone.

5. What action step will you take this week to apply what you learned about exporting?

I want to disciple someone, and have someone be willing to learn.

I will ask God for this person!

WELCOME II 15 MINUTES

Were you more of an obedient or disobedient child growing up?

Why do you think you were the way you were?

WITNESS II 10 MINUTES

What did you see God do this week?

WORSHIP II 10 MINUTES

Thank God together in prayer for what he did last week.

Use an iPod, guitar, etc. and sing a few songs together.

WORKS II 25 MINUTES

FISHING CHART
Update your FISHing chart with any new people you met this week or steps you took in the FISHing process.

BIG BLUE
Add your team's new friends to Big Blue. Put the list in the middle of the group and pray over your friends.

TOOLS
The leader should introduce "God's Heart for the Nations" (p. 127) and then demonstrate how to share it.

Pair up and practice "God's Heart for the Nations" with another teammate, giving each other feedback.

ACTIVITY
Turn to the Game Plan on the next page and fill in your goals for this week.

WORLD II 10 MINUTES

KNOW GOD'S WORLD: Muslim

There are 1.3 billion people in 1,344 Muslim people groups.[1]

They believe in one God, named Allah, and that Mohammad was his final prophet.

They believe if the good deeds done in life outweigh the bad deeds, Muslims go to Paradise when they die.

They respect Jesus as a good prophet but do not believe he is God.

SHARE HELPFUL RESOURCES
Report on this week's resource: Launch Global (launchglobal.org)

Assign next week's resource: Joshua Project (joshuaproject.net)

PRAY FOR THE NATIONS

WORD II 20 MINUTES

Share Matthew 9:37-38 with a partner.

Discuss the major learning points and application steps from your Daily Quiet Times (Day 7).

Discuss your answers to the Learning Questions for *Spiritual Multiplication in the Real World* (Ch. 9).

Close with prayer.

GAME PLAN FOR NEXT WEEK

3 HOURS *with Jesus*

Daily Quiet Times
Memorize Key Verse: 2 Corinthians 3:5-6

2 HOURS *with lost people*

Share God's Heart for the Nations
I will share God's Heart for the Nations with _____ people this week

My ministry partner this week will be _____

1 HOUR *with each other in prayer*

This week I will pray with _____

LEARNING ASSIGNMENT

Read *Spiritual Multiplication in the Real World* (Ch. 10) and answer the
Learning Questions

WEEK NINE

Chapter 10: You Can!

KEY VERSE

2 Corinthians 3:5-6
Not that we are sufficient in ourselves to claim anything as coming from us, but our sufficiency is from God, who has made us sufficient to be ministers of a new covenant, not of the letter but of the Spirit. For the letter kills, but the Spirit gives life.

SPIRITUAL MULTIPLICATION IN THE REAL WORLD

WORD: 1 Timothy 1:18, 4:11-16; 2 Timothy 1:6-7

In what ways was Paul empowering Timothy with his words in 1 Timothy 4:11-16?

He was encouraging Him that now is the time Live out the gift given, and do not hold back the name of God. Live as an example and shine as Christ's

To whom should you speak encouraging and empowering truth today?

All believers. We have a platform that we should no be ashamed of. God is true and faithful

WORSHIP

Praise God for what you saw about him in the Word today.

Today I thank God for...

I will worship God by obeying in the following ways this week:

Today I will trust God for...

▷ Learn this week's Key Verse.

WORD: Matthew 10:19-20, Acts 1:8

How did Jesus empower his disciples in these verses?

He has given us His spirit. We speak boldly of His own words. We dont have to worry about words. We will be his £ witness! full of him.

To whom should you speak encouraging and empowering truth today?

WORSHIP

Praise God for what you saw about him in the Word today.

Today I thank God for...

I will worship God by obeying in the following ways this week:

Today I will trust God for...

▷ Review this week's Key Verse.

DAILY QUIET TIMES || WEEK 9: DAY 3

WORD: Matthew 17:19-21, 21:21

How was Jesus empowering his disciples in these verses?

Have faith in Him. Do not doubt.
He is God and we have every
reason to believe that he can perform
miracles through us.

To whom should you speak encouraging and empowering truth today?

WORSHIP

Praise God for what you saw about him in the Word today.

Today I thank God for...

I will worship God by obeying in the following ways this week:

Today I will trust God for...

▷ Review this week's Key Verse.

WORD: Luke 10:19, Matthew 28:20

What can you learn about empowering from what Jesus said in these verses?

Authority - we have nothing to fear.

He is with us always

God is present, & he is what we need every moment

How will you apply these truths to your life and ministry?

WORSHIP

Praise God for what you saw about him in the Word today.

Today I thank God for...

I will worship God by obeying in the following ways this week:

Today I will trust God for...

▷ Review this week's Key Verse.

WORD: 2 Corinthians 3:5-6

In light of these verses, how should you think about your ability to minister to others?

How will you act upon this truth?

WORSHIP

Praise God for what you saw about him in the Word today.

Today I thank God for...

I will worship God by obeying in the following ways this week:

Today I will trust God for...

▷ Review this week's Key Verse.

WORD: Philippians 4:13, 2 Corinthians 12:9-10

How should these verses influence your thinking about what you attempt in ministry?

How will you act upon these truths?

WORSHIP

Praise God for what you saw about him in the Word today.

Today I thank God for...

I will worship God by obeying in the following ways this week:

Today I will trust God for...

▷ Review this week's Key Verse.

DAILY QUIET TIMES || WEEK 9: DAY 7

SUMMARY AND REFLECTION DAY

After looking over this week's quiet times, summarize what God has been teaching you.

What specific action will you take to apply what you have learned?

Did you really meet with Jesus this week, or did you just go through the motions?

WORSHIP

Praise God for what you saw about him in the Word this week.

Today I thank God for...

I will worship God by obeying in the following ways this week:

Today I will trust God for...

▷ Write out this week's Key Verse below:

SPIRITUAL MULTIPLICATION IN THE REAL WORLD (Chapter 10)

1. Many believers feel ill-equipped to disciple others because they think discipling others is something only a highly knowledgeable and wise person can do. The author presents a different view than this. Explain what you believe the author's view is and your reaction to it.

We learn from experience, we gain passion when we immerse ourself in His work and gain hunger to know and share the things of God.

2. Review the lies that Satan tells people mentioned in Chapter 10. What are the lies you find yourself believing most frequently?

I think I most frequently belief that I dont have enough time, or that I dont have the resources or what it takes to build anything even a disciple or church

3. If you knew for sure that God's power was upon you and that anything you attempted for him would succeed, what do you believe he would want you to attempt?

I believe he would want me to open up my life to build a church. an organic church full of multiplying believers experiencing the reality of God

WELCOME II 15 MINUTES

Who do you know who is most committed to fulfilling the Great Commission, and what is it that you see in his or her life that makes you select this person?

WITNESS II 10 MINUTES

What did you see God do this week?

WORSHIP II 10 MINUTES

Thank God together in prayer for what he did last week.

Take turns reading a few verses of Psalm 145, stopping to praise God for who he is and what he does.

WORKS II 25 MINUTES

FISHING CHART
Update your FISHing chart with any new people you met this week or steps you took in the FISHing process.

BIG BLUE
Add your team's new friends to Big Blue. Put the list in the middle of the group and pray over your friends.

TOOLS
The leader should introduce "Sharing the Vision of Multiplication" (p. 125) and then demonstrate how to share it.

Pair up and practice "Sharing the Vision of Multiplication" with another teammate, giving each other feedback.

ACTIVITY
Turn to the Game Plan on the next page and fill in your goals for this week.

WORLD II 10 MINUTES

KNOW GOD'S WORLD: Buddhists

There are 275 million people in 227 Buddhist people groups.[1]

They believe that suffering is caused by desire.

To end suffering, they must rid themselves of desire through meditation and multiple reincarnations.

The ultimate goal is to reach Nirvana, where suffering ends and the self ceases to exist.

SHARE HELPFUL RESOURCES
Report on this week's resource: Joshua Project (joshuaproject.net)

Assign next week's resource: The Traveling Team (thetravelingteam. org)

PRAY FOR THE NATIONS

WORD II 20 MINUTES

Share 2 Corinthians 3:5-6 with a partner.

Discuss the major learning points and application steps from your Daily Quiet Times (Day 7).

Discuss your answers to the Learning Questions for *Spiritual Multiplication in the Real World* (Ch. 10).

Close with prayer.

GAME PLAN FOR NEXT WEEK

3 HOURS *with Jesus*

Daily Quiet Times
Memorize Key Verse: Galatians 6:9

2 HOURS *with lost people*

This week, the evangelistic activity I will do is: _____
I will do an evangelistic activity with _____ people this week

Share the Vision for Spiritual Multiplication
I will share the Vision for Spiritual Multiplication with _____ people this week

My ministry partner this week will be _____

1 HOUR *with each other in prayer*

This week I will pray with _____

LEARNING ASSIGNMENT

Read *Spiritual Multiplication in the Real World* (Ch. 11) and answer the
Learning Questions

WEEK TEN

Chapter 11: From Vision to Reality

KEY VERSE

Galatians 6:9
And let us not grow weary of doing good, for in due season we will reap, if we do not give up.

WORD

Requirements for Multiplication	Observations about God

Mark 4

What does this passage teach will be required to see your vision of spiritual multiplication become a reality?

WORSHIP

Praise God for what you saw about him in the Word today.

Today I thank God for...

I will worship God by obeying in the following ways this week:

Today I will trust God for...

▷ Learn this week's Key Verse.

WORD

Requirements for Multiplication	Observations about God

John 15

What does this passage teach will be required to see your vision of spiritual multiplication become a reality?

WORSHIP

Praise God for what you saw about him in the Word today.

Today I thank God for...

I will worship God by obeying in the following ways this week:

Today I will trust God for...

▷ Review this week's Key Verse.

WORD: Matthew 6:24, 2 Timothy 2:4, John 12:20-26

What do these passages teach will be required to see your vision of spiritual multiplication become a reality?

What do you need to do to apply what is taught in these verses?

WORSHIP

Praise God for what you saw about him in the Word today.

Today I thank God for...

I will worship God by obeying in the following ways this week:

Today I will trust God for...

▷ Review this week's Key Verse.

WORD: Hebrews 4:14-16

What does this passage teach will be required to see your vision of spiritual multiplication become a reality?

What do you need to do to apply what is taught in these verses?

WORSHIP

Praise God for what you saw about him in the Word today.

Today I thank God for...

I will worship God by obeying in the following ways this week:

Today I will trust God for...

▷ Review this week's Key Verse.

WORD: Revelation 2:1-7

What does this passage teach will be required to see your vision of spiritual multiplication become a reality?

What do you need to do to apply what is taught in these verses?

WORSHIP

Praise God for what you saw about him in the Word today.

Today I thank God for...

I will worship God by obeying in the following ways this week:

Today I will trust God for...

▷ Review this week's Key Verse.

WORD: Galatians 6:9, 1 Corinthians 15:58

What do these passages teach will be required to see your vision of spiritual multiplication become a reality?

What do you need to do to apply what is taught in these verses?

WORSHIP

Praise God for what you saw about him in the Word today.

Today I thank God for...

I will worship God by obeying in the following ways this week:

Today I will trust God for...

▷ Review this week's Key Verse.

SUMMARY AND REFLECTION DAY

After looking over this week's quiet times, summarize what God has been teaching you.

What specific action will you take to apply what you have learned?

Did you really meet with Jesus this week, or did you just go through the motions?

WORSHIP

Praise God for what you saw about him in the Word this week.

Today I thank God for...

I will worship God by obeying in the following ways this week:

Today I will trust God for...

▷ Write out this week's Key Verse below:

SPIRITUAL MULTIPLICATION IN THE REAL WORLD (Chapter 11)

1. After reading about the direct relationship between one's time alone with God and one's fruitfulness in ministry, do you need to make any changes in your devotional practices? If so, what are they?

2. What "other visions" or "cares of the world" do you need to deal with if you are going to multiply your life?

3. Which of the "First Steps" do you need to take?

4. What are some of the things in your plan that you are trusting God to do through your life?

5. Whom are you going to ask to team up with you in the mission of disciple-making?

6. If you gave up on disciple-making one day in the future, what do you think would be the reason?

7. The author described our mission in this way, "As part of a disciple-making team, go and multiply disciple-making teams in all nations." Do you think explaining our mission in this way is helpful? Why or why not?

WELCOME II 15 MINUTES

Share how this group has helped you over the last nine weeks.

WITNESS II 10 MINUTES

What did you see God do this week?

WORSHIP II 10 MINUTES

Thank God together in prayer for what he did last week.

Use an iPod, guitar, etc. and sing a few songs together.

WORKS II 25 MINUTES

FISHING CHART
Update your FISHing chart with any new people you met this week or steps you took in the FISHing process.

BIG BLUE
Add your team's new friends to Big Blue. Spend an extended time praying for all of your friends on this list.

ACTIVITY
Discuss and fill out "My Disciple-Making Plan" on p. 129.

Discuss the future of your team.

WORLD II 10 MINUTES

KNOW GOD'S WORLD: Internationals

There are over 680,000 international students who study and live in the United States every year.[5]

Sixty percent of international students come from the 10/40 Window.

Forty percent of the world's 220 Heads of State once studied in the US.

Eighty percent of these students will return to their countries having never been invited to an American home.[4]

SHARE HELPFUL RESOURCES
Report on this week's resource: The Traveling Team (thetravelingteam.org)

PRAY FOR THE NATIONS

WORD II 20 MINUTES

Share Galatians 6:9 with a partner.

Discuss the major learning points and application steps from your Daily Quiet Times (Day 7).

Discuss your answers to the Learning Questions for *Spiritual Multiplication in the Real World* (Ch. 11).

Close with prayer.

APPENDIX

FISHING CHART

#	Name	FIND			INTEREST					SHARE					HELP	
		Interests	Felt Needs	Attitude Toward Jesus	Testimony	Answered Prayer Stories	Community	Prayer for their needs	Jesus Story	Discovery Bible Study	Gospel Presentation	Something to Read	Ask for a Decision	Deal with Barriers		
1	Sidney															
2																
3																
4																
5																
6																
7																
8																
9																
10																

FISHING CHART

		FIND			INTEREST				SHARE				HELP	
#	Name	Interests	Felt Needs	Attitude Toward Jesus	Testimony	Answered Prayer Stories	Community	Prayer for their needs	Jesus Story	Discovery Bible Study	Gospel Presentation	Something to Read	Ask for a Decision	Deal with Barriers
1														
2														
3														
4														
5														
6														
7														
8														
9														
10														

MY STORY II INTEREST-CREATING TESTIMONY

I first sensed my need for Jesus when…

What made me most interested in Jesus was…

His unconditional love for others regardless of what they have or havent done.

I finally decided to trust Jesus and follow him when I realized that…

Since I entered into a relationship with Jesus, I have changed

From: *empty feeling despite my actions*   To: *full of joy and purpose*

From: *living in guilt from my failures*   To: *believing I'm forgiven and free from my past mistakes*

Jesus helps me in my daily life by…

I have seen God answer my prayers in some pretty cool ways, like the time…

_____ have you ever considered learning about how to follow Jesus?

When meeting new people, the easiest way to begin getting to know them is by asking questions. It is usually best to start by asking biographical questions before asking more personal questions about their interests and needs. Take a minute to read over the following example questions. Then take turns practicing asking questions and moving the conversation from biographical to interests to needs.

1. **Biographical questions:**

Where are you from?

Where do you live now?

What do you do?

Tell me about your family.

2. **Interests questions:** (Hopefully, these questions will help you find some ways you can spend time together in the future.)

Do you have any hobbies or favorite sports?

What is your favorite thing to do in your free time?

3. **Needs questions:**

I try to pray for the needs of people I meet. Is there anything specific I can pray for you?

GLOSSARY

THE LEGEND OF BIG BLUE

In 2007, a dedicated group of believers in Iowa began to meet as a missional community. A cornerstone of their weekly meetings was a time of prayer for the lost. Names of lost friends were written on a leftover piece of blue flooring material, which was then laid in the middle of the room to be prayed over. Each week, as members recalled people they had met, new names were added to the list. A time of intense prayer would follow as disciples got on their knees to pray over "Big Blue." As these groups multiplied and spread to other states, so did the inclusion of Big Blue. Get a blue piece of fabric or poster board and join the movement!

MATTHEW PARTY

A Matthew Party is a get-together planned for people who need to meet Jesus. We get the name from Matthew, the tax collector, who held a reception in his home for people to come meet Jesus. One of the goals of this event is to allow our lost friends to experience the difference Christ makes in a community of believers. It is important that we aren't outnumbered, as seeing Christ-centered community in action is the goal behind this gathering. We want them to see the love we have for one another. A Matthew Party can be a dinner, a game night, bowling, ice skating, some sort of cultural activity, etc. The important thing is allowing our lost friends to spend time with a group of believers.

LUKE 5:29-32 (ESV)

And Levi [Matthew] made him [Jesus] a great feast in his house, and there was a large company of tax collectors and others reclining at table with them. And the Pharisees and their scribes grumbled at his disciples, saying, "Why do you eat and drink with tax collectors and sinners?"

And Jesus answered them, "Those who are well have no need of a physician, but those who are sick. I have not come to call the righteous but sinners to repentance."

JOHN 13:35

By this all people will know that you are my disciples, if you have love for one another.

If you need a video demonstration of The Bridge, several good versions can be found online.

SHARING THE VISION II FOR MULTIPLICATION (FILLED IN)

YOUR POTENTIAL IMPACT

If you only discipled two people per year and taught them to teach others to multiply each year, you could multiply over _3 Billion_ disciples in just twenty years.

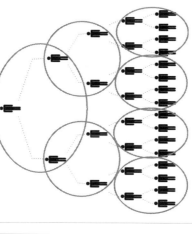

☐ Draw circles around groups of disciples and discuss the importance of multiplying not only disciples, but disciple-making teams.

WHAT ACTION WILL YOU TAKE?

☐ I will seek out someone to disciple me.
☐ I will seek out people to disciple.

WHAT PAUL DID

"And what you have heard from me in the presence of many witnesses entrust to faithful men who will be able to teach others also."

2 Timothy 2:2

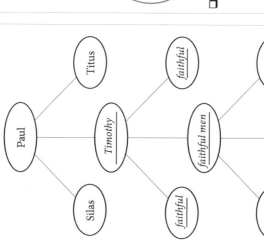

WHAT JESUS DID

Jesus

The Twelve

Peter
James
John

Inner _Circle_

WHAT JESUS COMMANDED

"Therefore go and _make_ _disciples_ of _all_ _nations_, baptizing them in the name of the Father and of the Son and of the Holy Spirit."

Matthew 28:19

WHAT JESUS PROMISED

"Others, like seed sown on good soil, hear the word, accept it, and produce a crop— some _30_, some _60_, some _100_ times what was sown."

Mark 4:20

YOUR POTENTIAL IMPACT

If you only discipled two people per year and taught them to teach others to multiply each year, you could multiply over 3 disciples in just twenty years.

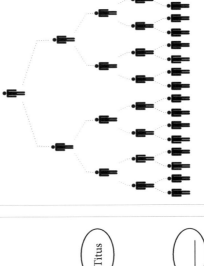

☐ Draw circles around groups of disciples and discuss the importance of multiplying not only disciples, but disciple-making teams.

WHAT ACTION WILL YOU TAKE?

☐ I will seek out someone to disciple me.

☐ I will seek out people to disciple.

WHAT PAUL DID

"And what you have heard from me in the presence of many witnesses entrust to faithful men who will be able to teach others also."

2 Timothy 2:2

Paul

Titus

Silas

WHAT JESUS DID

The Twelve

Peter
James
John

Inner _____

WHAT JESUS COMMANDED

"Therefore go and _____ of _____, baptizing them in the name of the Father and of the Son and of the Holy Spirit."

Matthew 28:19

WHAT JESUS PROMISED

"Others, like seed sown on good soil, hear the word, accept it, and produce a crop—some _____, some _____, some _____ times what was sown."

Mark 4:20

1 THE GRAND NARRATIVE

1. Commission to multiply God's image bearers in all the earth: **Genesis 1:28**

2. Image marred: **Genesis 3:15**

3. People Groups Formed: **Genesis 11:8**

4. God's plan to bless all nations through Abraham's Children: **Genesis 12:2-3**

5. Example of an Old Testament imperative to preach to the nations: **1 Chronicles 16:24**

6. All believers are children of Abraham and have the same blessings and responsibilities: **Galatians 3:7-9**

7. The gospel of the kingdom and the demonstration of its power went to the Jews first: **Matthew 10:6-8**

8. The blessing is supposed to spread to all nations: **Acts 1:8**

9. Jesus has commanded all of his followers to spread his kingdom to the nations (ethne): **Matthew 28:18-20**

10. We should make the unreached our ambition: **Romans 15:20**

11. Jesus ransomed all nations: **Revelation 5:9**

12. All nations will be in heaven: **Revelation 7:9**

2 THE GREAT IMBALANCE

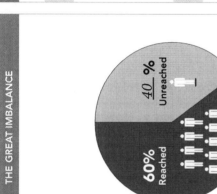

60%
Reached

_40_ %
Unreached

The average American spends **$20 per week** on coffee.

The average American Christian gives _1.5 cents_ to the unreached each week.

3 YOUR PART

WHAT DO YOU THINK IS YOUR MOST STRATEGIC ROLE?

1. Go
2. Give
3. Pray
4. _Welcome_
5. _Mobilize_
6. _Other:_ _____

WHAT DO YOU THINK IS YOUR MOST STRATEGIC LOCATION?

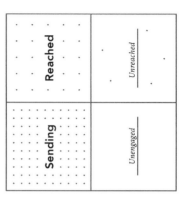

Sending · · · Reached

Unengaged

Unreached

WHAT DO YOU THINK IS YOUR MOST STRATEGIC NEXT STEP?

1 THE GRAND NARRATIVE

1. Commission to multiply God's image bearers in all the earth: **Genesis 1:28**

2. Image marred: **Genesis 3:15**

3. People Groups Formed: **Genesis 11:8**

4. God's plan to bless all nations through Abraham's Children: **Genesis 12:2-3**

5. Example of an Old Testament imperative to preach to the nations: **1 Chronicles 16:24**

6. All believers are children of Abraham and have the same blessings and responsibilities: **Galatians 3:7-9**

7. The gospel of the kingdom and the demonstration of its power went to the Jews first: **Matthew 10:6-8**

8. The blessing is supposed to spread to all nations: **Acts 1:8**

9. Jesus has commanded all of his followers to spread his kingdom to the nations (*ethne*): **Matthew 28:18-20**

10. We should make the unreached our ambition: **Romans 15:20**

11. Jesus ransomed all nations: **Revelation 5:9**

12. All nations will be in heaven: **Revelation 7:9**

2 THE GREAT IMBALANCE

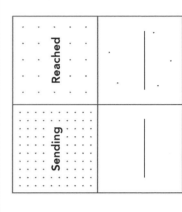

60%
Reached

___%
Unreached

The average American spends **$20 per week** on coffee.

The average American Christian gives _____ to the unreached each week.

3 YOUR PART

WHAT DO YOU THINK IS YOUR MOST STRATEGIC ROLE?

1. Go
2. Give
3. Pray
4. _____
5. _____
6. _____

WHAT DO YOU THINK IS YOUR MOST STRATEGIC LOCATION?

Sending | Reached

WHAT DO YOU THINK IS YOUR MOST STRATEGIC NEXT STEP?

MY DISCIPLE-MAKING PLAN

VISION: I would like to see the following vision become a reality:

TRUSTING GOD: I am trusting God to do the following:

Before I die:

In the next three years:

In the next twelve months:

In the next three months:

I am claiming the following promises from God's Word:

SHARING THE VISION: I will ask the following people to join me in the vision and to speak into it:

PIN IT UP: I will put a visual reminder in the following places:

FOUNDATIONS:
MISSIONAL COMMUNITY GUIDEBOOK

AN ESTABLISHING TOOL

This resource is designed to lead new believers into missional community and outreach while establishing them in the foundations of the faith. Together, disciples learn how to grow spiritually and bear fruit as obedient followers of Christ. Foundations is a proven tool to practically build up your disciples in the basics of a Christ-centered life while they reach out to others as a community. It will solidify their faith through the study of the following lessons:

Week 1: My Story

Week 2: The Gospel

Week 3: Assurance of Salvation

Week 4: Following Christ as Lord

Week 5: Living in Grace

Week 6: Purpose in Life

Week 7: Quiet Time

Week 8: The Word

Week 9: Prayer

Week 10: Life in the Spirit

Week 11: Perseverance in Suffering

BULK PRICING AVAILABLE AT SPIRITUALMULTIPLICATION.ORG

ENDNOTES

1   *The Task Remaining* by Ralph D. Winter and Bruce A. Koch, *Perspectives on the World Christian Movement, Reader.* 4th ed. William Carey Library, 2009, p.531-546. *www.missionbooks.org*

2   Joshua Project, *www.joshuaproject.org*

3   *The Coming Revolution: Because Status Quo Missions Won't Finish the Job* by Mark R. Baxter, Tate Publishing, 2007, p.12.

4   The Traveling Team, *www.thetravelingteam.org*

5   Statistics from The Institute of International Education, Inc. *www.iie.org*